THE LEFT BANK LOOK

EASY PARISIAN-CHIC PROJECTS FOR YOUR HOME AND CLOTHES

ANNE HUBERT

THE LEFT BANK LOOK

EASY PARISIAN-CHIC PROJECTS FOR YOUR HOME AND CLOTHES

Photography by Coco Amardeil

Watson-Guptill Publications/New York

745.5

Anne Hubert

CONTENTS

INSPIRATIONS

MY DESIGNS ARE INSPIRED BY IMAGES AND
OBJECTS GATHERED IN THE COURSE OF DAY-TO-
DAY LIFE, MANY OF WHICH FILL MY HOME. HERE'S
A PEEK AT WHAT YOU'D FIND IF YOU CAME OVER:
PHOTOS AND TRINKETS DECORATING THE WALLS,
TRAVEL JOURNALS FILLED WITH SOUVENIRS, A
PINK EIFFEL TOWER, OLD PHOTOGRAPHS I CAN'T
BEAR TO THROW AWAY, TINS OF CRAFT SUPPLIES,
BOOKS FROM ALL OVER THE WORLD, TROMPE-
L'OEIL DESIGNS...LITTLE TREASURES THAT MAKE
UP THE WHOLE OF MY SECRET UNIVERSE.

A BLANK SLATE

WE ALL WANT OUR T-SHIRTS, BED LINENS, AND TOTE BAGS TO LOOK DIFFERENT FROM
EVERYONE ELSE'S. IN THIS AGE OF MASS PRODUCTION THERE'S AN EVEN GREATER NEED
TO PROJECT A MORE PERSONAL STYLE. BUT WHO HAS THE TIME—OR PATIENCE—FOR
GRAND CRAFT PROJECTS, ESPECIALLY WITH NO GUARANTEE HOW THEY WILL TURN OUT?
THIS BOOK IS A COLLECTION OF VERY SIMPLE IDEAS THAT ARE QUICK AND EASY TO DO,
INSPIRED BY MY LIFE AND WORK IN PARIS. WITH MINIMUM COST AND MAXIMUM EFFECT,
THEY WILL TRANSFORM PLAIN, EVERYDAY BASICS INTO LOVELY, MORE PERSONAL ITEMS.

THE TECHNIQUES

DYEING

Always buy a good-quality fabric dye and follow the manufacturer's instructions on the package step by step. I used Dylon® brand for the projects in this book, but there are many other good brands out there as well (see Resources on page 63 for options available in the U.S.).

• The amount of dye needed depends on the dry weight of fabric to be dyed, so don't forget to weigh it before you go out and buy the dye. Packages of dye usually contain enough to treat 8 ounces to 1 pound (250–500g) of fabric, but you can always add a T-shirt to make up the weight if needed.

• If the fabric weighs more than the weight indicated on the package, the resulting color will be lighter. If it weighs less, the color will be darker.

• You may need to add salt when using some dyes—check manufacturer's instructions.

• Make sure your fabric is suitable for dyeing. Natural, washable fabrics work best, such as cotton, linen, and wool, but some synthetics also accept dye, including rayon, nylon, acetate, and fiber-blends with more than 60 percent cotton. Fabrics that do not accept dye include blends with 50 percent or more polyester, as well as acrylic, fabrics with fiberglass, metallic fibers, or special finishes, and those washable only in cold water or labeled "dry clean only." If you have any doubts about whether your fabric will accept dye, test a swatch first.

• Make sure the fabric is clean, without any stains or marks, as dyeing does not cover defects. If the fabric to be dyed is stained or yellowed, treat it with a stain- or color-remover first.

• You can create your own unique colors by mixing more than one color dye. Always test the mixture by dyeing a sample of fabric by hand first, before doing a whole machine load.

• Take into account the original color of the fabric—yellow fabric treated with blue dye will turn green.

• Always make sure you wear rubber gloves when using dyes.

• And finally, to answer to the inevitable question about whether it's safe to use your washing machine for this purpose: after dyeing, simply run a few old rags through a complete wash cycle with hot water, detergent, and 1 cup chlorine bleach, and all trace of the dye will be gone.

• Always wash the dyed fabric separately for the first time.

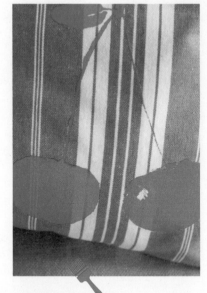

STENCILING

• To create a stencil from a design in this book, photocopy the design in black and white at the size indicated. Using repositionable spray adhesive, stick the copy onto a piece of thin cardboard or plastic film, then cut away the inside of the shape as accurately as possible using a craft knife.

• Place the stencil on the fabric and anchor with masking tape. If you are working on a cushion or bedsheet, slip an extra sheet of cardboard under the top layer of fabric, to prevent seepage. Use a stencil brush or sponge to apply fabric paint inside the stencil, using light dabbing motions. Don't overload the brush or the dye may bleed under the stencil. Remove the stencil before the pattern is completely dry, then let dry for at least 4 more hours.

• To fix your design, cover it with a piece of clean fabric and press with a hot iron for 2 minutes.

• If you are stenciling onto printed fabric, start with a layer of white fabric paint to cover the pattern inside the stencil. Remove the stencil and fix the paint, as above. Then replace the stencil and repeat with your colored fabric paint.

• Stenciled fabric can be machine washed at 86° F (30° C).

TRANSFERRING IMAGES

At an imaging center

The simplest way to transfer or copy an image onto fabric is to take the fabric and image to an imaging center—the kind that transfers designs onto T-shirts. They will scan the image and print it onto your garment or fabric, either by printing it onto transfer paper first and heat-bonding it to the fabric, or by using a computer-controlled plotter to cut the image out of a special foil and then fusing it with the fabric. To save time, provide them with a scan of your image on a CD.

At home

You can also transfer designs yourself, using transfer paper or a transfer medium (see Resources on page 63). To use transfer paper, print or photocopy your image right onto the paper. Lay the paper facedown on your fabric, iron the reverse side, then peel off the backing paper. To use transfer medium, first photocopy your image if you don't want to ruin the original. Spread some medium on the image and place it facedown on the fabric. Let dry overnight.

CUTTING RAW EDGES

A raw edge is simply an edge left unhemmed, so the fabric frays a little. This does away with the chore of hemming and, happily, creates a stylish effect at the same time. If you want to limit the amount of fraying, do a row of stitching along the edge. Note that it's very important to have a pair of scissors you use only for fabric. As soon as you use them to cut paper, they will no longer work as well on fabric.

The next day, wet the back of the image, rub off the paper, apply a sealing coat, and your fabric is ready. Always bear in mind that images will be reproduced backward (as if reflected in a mirror), so avoid ones with text. Let dry for 72 hours, then machine wash the printed fabric, inside out, at 86° F (30° C). Refer to transfer paper or medium packaging for individual manufacturer's instructions.

SEWING

Sewing can be used to appliqué one fabric onto another, to join two pieces of fabric, or to "draw" a design or shape with stitching. Some projects in this book use "freehand" machine sewing to create a loose-looking design. The more haphazard the stitching, the more stylish the result. If you want, first draw the design onto your fabric with tailor's chalk or a fabric pencil before starting to sew. But don't worry—if you don't like the finished look, you can always undo the sewing with a seam ripper and start over.

FOUR WAYS TO GIVE THROW PILLOWS A FRESH NEW LOOK

It's time to do something about those dreary pillows taking place of honor on the sofa. Start with any neutral-colored pillow cover, either store-bought or created yourself. Then choose your favorite design and get to work.

01 PILLOWS

DANCING SHOES

• PILLOW COVER

For this project you'll need a professional image transfer service.
Take this book to an imaging center that makes T-shirts. Ask them to apply the shoe design shown opposite in whatever finish you want to your fabric.

Actual size of design: 7½ inches (19 cm)

A—

MES AMIS

• PICTURE(S) OF YOUR FAVORITE PEOPLE
• PILLOW COVER
• MASKING TAPE
• WHITE FABRIC PAINT
• PAINTBRUSH
• TRANSFER MEDIUM OR PAPER
• IRON

Print or photocopy the picture in the size required.
Use masking tape to mark where on the fabric you want the picture.
Paint the area with white fabric paint. Remove the tape, let dry for 2 hours, then fix the paint with a hot iron (see page 10). Follow the instructions on the transfer paper or medium to transfer your image onto the area painted white. Alternatively, take the image to an imaging center and let them do the work for you (see page 11 for further information).
Let dry 72 hours. After that, you can machine wash the finished fabric at 86° F (30° C), but make sure you turn it inside out first.

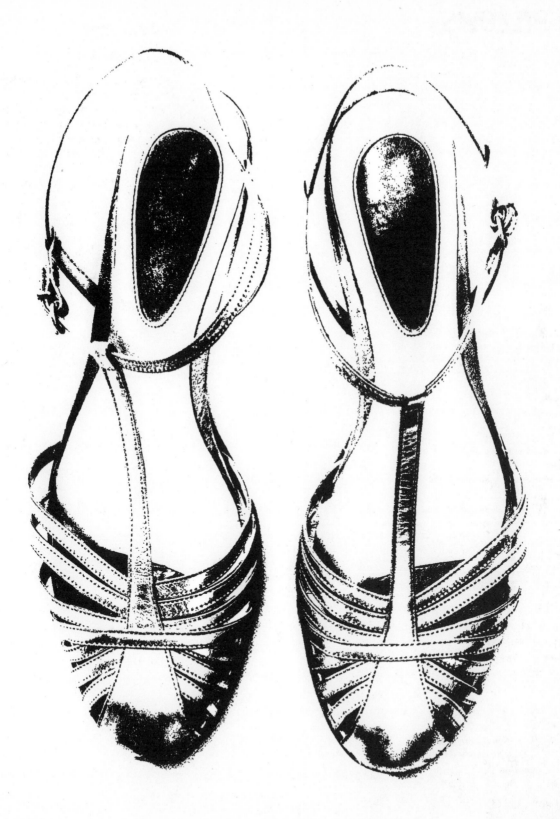

C —
RIPE CHERRIES

- PILLOW COVER
- 2 SHEETS OF THIN CARDBOARD, APPROX. 9 x 10 in. (23 x 26 cm)
- WHITE FABRIC PAINT (FOR PRINTED OR DARK FABRICS ONLY)
- BRIGHT PINK FABRIC PAINT (WE USED DYLON IN FLUORESCENT PINK NO. 20)
- REPOSITIONABLE SPRAY ADHESIVE
- CRAFT KNIFE
- MASKING TAPE
- STENCIL BRUSH OR SPONGE
- IRON

Photocopy the cherry design at 115 percent. Stick it to a sheet of cardboard using spray adhesive, then use a craft knife to cut out the inside of the design as accurately as possible. Position the stencil on the pillow cover, anchor it with masking tape, and slip the second sheet of cardboard inside the cover to stop paint from penetrating through the fabric. If your fabric has a printed design, as shown here, start with a layer of white paint. (If your fabric is solid, skip this step.) Apply the white fabric paint with the stencil brush or sponge using light dabbing motions. Don't overload the brush or the paint will bleed beneath the stencil. When you're done, remove the stencil. Let dry at least 4 hours. Place a clean piece of fabric over the design and fix with a hot iron for 2 minutes.

Next, position the stencil back in the same place and apply a second coat of paint in bright pink.

Remove the stencil before the design is quite dry. Let dry completely, then place a clean piece of fabric over the design and fix with a hot iron for 2 minutes.

The finished pillow cover can be machine washed at 86° F (30° C).

Actual size of cherry design: 7½ inches (19 cm)

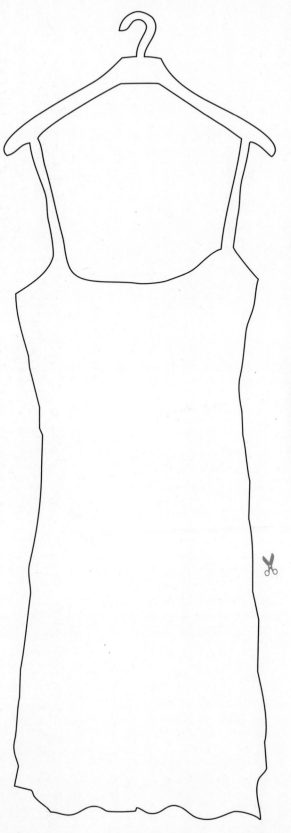

D —
FLORAL CHEMISE

- PILLOW COVER
- PIECE OF FLOWERY FABRIC, APPROX. 6 x 15 in. (15 x 38 cm)
- REPOSITIONABLE SPRAY ADHESIVE
- STRAIGHT PINS
- BRIGHT PINK THREAD
- FABRIC SCISSORS
- SEWING MACHINE

Photocopy the dress design at 175 percent. Lightly spray the back of the photocopy with adhesive and stick it to the wrong side of the fabric. Cut out the design. Gently pull the photocopy off the fabric. Pin the cut-out dress shape to the pillow cover, right side up. Sew around the edges of the dress appliqué with pink thread, but don't be too neat—the more the edges fray the better it looks.

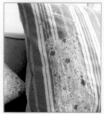

For a closer view of the project, see page 2.

Actual size of dress appliqué: 14½ inches (37 cm)

02 CURTAINS

02 CURTAINS

A —
IN MY SHOES

- SHEER WHITE COTTON CURTAIN PANEL
- INSTANT PHOTOS OF YOUR FAVORITE SHOES (OR OTHER FAVORITE OBJECT)
- MASKING TAPE

Choose your photos.
Decide where you want them to appear on the panel and mark the places with masking tape. Take everything to an imaging center and ask them to transfer the images to your fabric as marked.

Actual size of photos: 7 inches (18 cm) each

B —
SHEER AND LACY

- SHEER WHITE COTTON CURTAIN PANEL
- 9 WHITE CLOTH DOILIES
- STRAIGHT PINS
- BRIGHT PINK THREAD
- SEWING MACHINE

Lay the panel out flat, right side up, and pin the doilies to it in a random fashion. Using a sewing machine and pink thread, run a haphazard line of stitching down the whole vertical length of the panel, passing through each doily to secure it in place. Run a similar line of stitching across the width of the panel.

03 T-SHIRTS

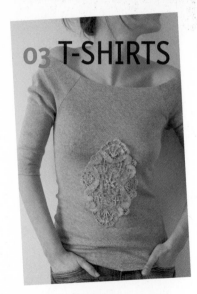

A COLLECTION OF CUSTOMIZED T-SHIRTS

Get all your tees out from your dresser, your closet, under the bed—wherever they may be stashed—and arm yourself with a pair of scissors and loads of confidence. You're going to cut, sew, and appliqué your way to a whole new level of everyday chic.

03 T-SHIRTS

A—
LOW-CUT AND LACY

- PLAIN T-SHIRT WITH THREE-QUARTER-LENGTH SLEEVES
- WHITE LACE PLACEMAT OR LARGE DOILY
- FABRIC DYE TO MATCH THE T-SHIRT
- STRAIGHT PINS
- BRIGHTLY COLORED THREAD OF YOUR CHOICE
- FABRIC SCISSORS
- SEWING NEEDLE OR SEWING MACHINE

Dye the lace the same color as the T-shirt, following directions on the dye package. Let dry.

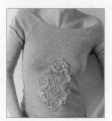

Cut away the neckband to form a scoop neckline, as shown.
Pin the lace to the front of the tee, as shown, and stitch in place, either by hand or machine, using small stitches and brightly colored thread.

B—
LITTLE BLACK TEE

- SHORT-SLEEVE BLACK T-SHIRT
- TAILOR'S CHALK OR FABRIC PENCIL
- FABRIC SCISSORS

Going out for the evening but can't find a thing to wear? Here's a super-quick fix with a ton of street style.
Put on the T-shirt and stand in front of a mirror. Decide how low you want the v-neck to go and make a mark with the chalk or pencil. Now decide how wide you want to the v-neck to be and make a mark on each side along the shoulder seams.
Lay the T-shirt on a flat surface and draw a V from the center mark to the marks on the shoulder seams. Cut your v-neck along this line, as shown.
Draw a line from each armhole seam to the outer edge of the sleeve, as shown, and cut.

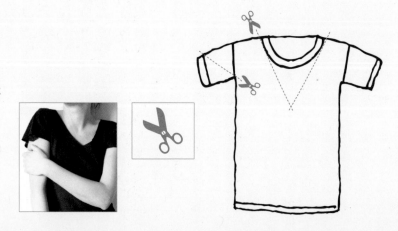

C —
BASIC TEE, REVISITED

- SHORT-SLEEVE T-SHIRT WITH CREW NECK
- FABRIC SCISSORS

Cut away the bulk of the neckband and sleeve hems, as shown.

D —
GATHERED SLEEVES

- SHORT-SLEEVE T-SHIRT WITH CREW NECK
- CONTRASTING BRIGHTLY COLORED THREAD
- FABRIC SCISSORS
- SEWING MACHINE

Sew a line of machine stitching along one side of the shoulder seam, about ¼ inch from the seam, starting at the neckband. When you reach the sleeve, continue stitching, gathering the fabric as you sew. Sew a second line of stitching along the other side of the seam to match.

Repeat with the other sleeve. For a modern look, trim away the bulk of the neckband.

E —
LE FLIRT

- PLAIN TANK TOP
- PIECE OF FLOWERY FABRIC
- STRAIGHT PINS
- THREAD THAT MATCHES FABRIC
- FABRIC SCISSORS
- SEWING MACHINE

Cut two strips of flowery fabric, each 29 x 4 inches (74 x 10 cm). Pin each strip around an armhole with about 2 inches of fabric extending out, pleating as you go. Concentrate the pleats at the top of the armhole and space them more widely near the armpit.

Machine stitch the strips in place, using a zigzag stitch so the seams stay flexible. If necessary, trim the strips to neaten.

03 T-SHIRTS

F —
TWIN SET

- PLAIN T-SHIRT WITH THREE-QUARTER-LENGTH SLEEVES
- PLAIN TANK TOP
- TAILOR'S CHALK OR FABRIC PENCIL
- FABRIC SCISSORS

Lay the T-shirt on a flat surface, face up. Using tailor's chalk, draw a line from the center of the neck straight down to the hem and cut along the top layer to create a cardigan. Wear it over the tank.

Simple chic! Fasten the cardigan with a jeweled brooch for a touch of bohemian glamour.

G —
DANCER'S WRAP

- PLAIN LONG-SLEEVE T-SHIRT WITH CREW NECK
- PLAIN TANK TOP
- TAILOR'S CHALK OR FABRIC PENCIL
- 2 LENGTHS OF RIBBON IN CONTRASTING COLORS, EACH 32 in. (81 cm)
- STRAIGHT PINS
- FABRIC SCISSORS
- SEWING MACHINE

Put on the long-sleeve T-shirt and draw a horizontal line 2 inches (5 cm) below the bust. Lay the tee on a flat surface, face up. Cut away everything below the line. Now draw another line, going from the center of the neckline straight down to the bottom, and cut along only the top layer. Put on the resulting bolero and stand in front of a mirror. Draw whatever neckline you prefer with the chalk or pencil.

It's best to cut the neckline a little at a time and try it on after each cutting. When the shape is right for you, start at the side seams and pin each ribbon along either side of the front hem so they meet in the center. Sew the ribbons down. Leave the rest of each ribbon dangling free. Wear the wrap over the tank, with the ribbons wrapped and tied in back.

H —
APPLIQUÉD TEE

- PLAIN T-SHIRT WITH THREE-QUARTER-LENGTH SLEEVES
- PLAIN T-SHIRT OR TANK TOP OF SAME COLOR TO CUT UP
- STRAIGHT PINS
- BRIGHT PINK THREAD
- FABRIC SCISSORS
- SEWING MACHINE

Get the tee or tank you're planning to cut up and lay it on a flat surface, face up. Draw a horizontal line between the bases of the armhole seams and cut across, leaving a simple tube.

Put on the tee with three-quarter-length sleeves, then layer the cut tube on top, pulling it down to bust level. Carefully pin in place.

Cut 3 circles from the scrap fabric left from the first tee, sized 1 ½, 2 ½, and 3 inches in diameter (4, 6, and 8 cm). Stack the circles by size, with the biggest on the bottom. Position the stack where the two T-shirts meet on the left-hand side and pin in place. Carefully take off the tees.

Using the pink thread, sew haphazard lines of stitching across the stack to fix it in place. Secure the layered tees with a few stitches under the arms and sew an "x" at the back where the tube and T-shirt join to keep the whole thing together.

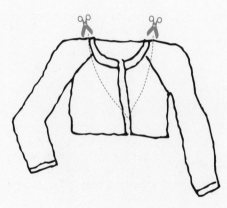

BAGS

REVAMP YOUR GEAR

You know those old, uninspired bags you've left hanging in your closet for too long? It's time to restyle and rejuvenate them!

04 BAGS

A—
BON VOYAGE

- CANVAS BAG
- FABRIC DYE (WE MIXED DYLON BEIGE NO. 10 AND BABY PINK NO. 07)
- IMAGE TRANSFER MEDIUM OR TRANSFER PAPER
- POSTCARD

Dye the bag following manufacturer's instructions on the package. Let dry.
Photocopy the postcard (if there is any text on the postcard, photocopy as a mirror image).
Follow instructions for image transfer medium or transfer paper to apply your postcard image to the bag.
Alternatively, take the bag and image to an imaging center and let them do the work for you (see page 11 for further information).
Hand wash only; do not iron or dry clean.

B—
SPRINGTIME IN PARIS

- CANVAS BAG
- FABRIC DYE (WE USED DYLON PEACOCK BLUE NO. 22)
- 10 APPLIQUÉ PATCHES (WE USED SILVER CHERRIES)
- STRAIGHT PINS
- BRIGHT PINK THREAD
- SEWING MACHINE OR NEEDLE

Dye the bag following manufacturer's instructions on the package. Let dry.
Pin the appliqué patches onto the bag, positioning them as you like, then sew a simple line of stitches across the center of each to fix in place.

C—
WHAT'S IN MY BAG?

- CANVAS BAG
- FABRIC DYE (WE USED DYLON ALMOND GREEN NO. 57)

Dye the bag following manufacturer's instructions on the package. Let dry.
Photocopy the design shown opposite at 125 percent, or just take the book to an imaging center and ask them to apply the design to the bag in fluorescent pink flock.

Actual size of design: 7¾ x 10¾ inches (20 x 27 cm)

05 KITCHEN LINENS

A —
SALON DISH TOWEL

Breathe new life into a kitchen
classic with fun, graphic motifs.

JEUDI: LAPIN À LA CASSEROLE

B—
FRENCH BISTRO TABLECLOTH
Create a statement with gingham and
turn your kitchen into a Parisian café.

C —
COLORFUL TABLECLOTHS AND NAPKINS

Your dining table won't know what hit it!

05 KITCHEN LINENS

A—
SALON DISH TOWEL

- PLAIN, NEUTRAL-COLORED DISH TOWEL
- PIECE OF THIN CARDBOARD
- FABRIC PAINT IN BLUE, PINK, AND BLACK (WE USED DYLON TURQUOISE NO. 28, FLUORESCENT PINK NO. 20, AND BLACK NO. 11)
- REPOSITIONABLE SPRAY ADHESIVE
- CRAFT KNIFE
- MASKING TAPE
- STENCIL BRUSH OR SPONGE
- IRON

Photocopy the designs shown here at 100 percent. Spray the backs with adhesive and stick them onto the cardboard. Use a craft knife to cut out the insides of the shapes, making your stencils.

Lay the dish towel flat, face up. Secure a stencil to it with masking tape. Apply the fabric paint with a stencil brush, using light dabbing motions. Carefully remove stencil when almost dry, then let dry completely. Repeat with the other two stencils, creating your tableau.

When you're done, lay a piece of plain fabric on top of your design and fix with a hot iron. You can machine wash the dish towel as needed.

The simple designs shown here were taken from children's stickers published by Editions Lito, drawn by Kaori Souvignet. There are many other designs out there—choose whichever ones you like best.

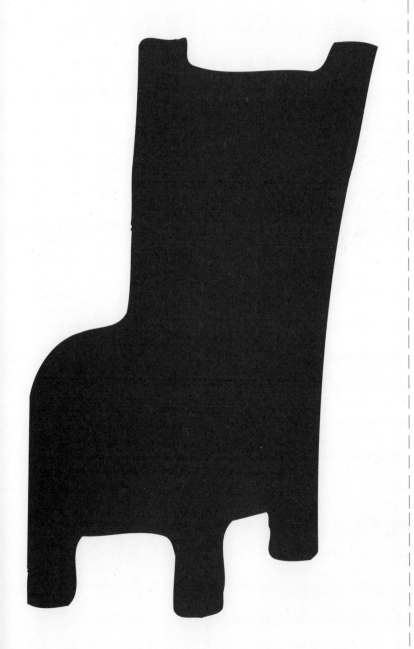

C —
COLORFUL TABLECLOTHS
AND NAPKINS

- PLAIN LINEN OR COTTON TABLECLOTH
- PLAIN LINEN OR COTTON NAPKINS
(THEY DON'T HAVE TO MATCH)
- FABRIC DYE (QUANTITY DEPENDS ON
THE WEIGHT OF FABRIC; WE USED DYLON
FABRIC DYE IN ALMOND GREEN NO. 57
FOR THE TABLECLOTH, AND STEEL GRAY
NO. 32, OLIVE GREEN NO. 34, PEACOCK
BLUE NO. 22, AND CHINA BLUE NO. 14 FOR
THE NAPKINS)

Fabric dye makes it easy to update old linen, whether to give it new life or just for the pleasure of bringing color to the table. And so what if the napkins are all different colors? So much the better. Choose a range of colors (take inspiration from your wallpaper, or your latest favorite outfit) and dye them according to the manufacturer's instructions on the package.

05 KITCHEN LINENS

B —

FRENCH BISTRO TABLECLOTH

- WHITE TABLECLOTH OR PIECE OF WHITE FABRIC, 2¾ YARDS (2.5 m), OR WHATEVER SIZE FITS YOUR TABLE
- PIECE OF RED COTTON GINGHAM, 8 x 36 in. (20 x 90 cm)
- DOUBLE-SIDED FUSIBLE INTERFACING, 8 x 36 in. (20 x 90 cm)
- REPOSITIONABLE SPRAY ADHESIVE
- WAX PAPER
- IRON
- BRIGHT PINK THREAD
- CRAFT KNIFE AND/OR FABRIC SCISSORS
- SEWING MACHINE

Photocopy the words shown here at 145 percent (or print out your own words). Lightly spray the back of the photocopy with adhesive and lay the gingham fabric onto it, right side down. Now lightly spray one side of the interfacing with adhesive and lay that onto the back of the gingham. Use the craft knife and/or fabric scissors to cut out each letter. Carefully pull away the photocopy. Place the letters, with the right side of the gingham fabric facing up, in a line down the middle of the tablecloth fabric, slightly off center.

Cover the letters with wax paper and press with a hot iron to fuse the interfacing to the fabric. Press firmly with the iron, making sure the letters stay put.

Finish with two rows of fairly irregular machine stitching across the letters, using the pink thread.

The tablecloth can be machine washed at 104° F (40° C).

Actual height of each letter: 2½ inches (6 cm)

ALA
CASSE
ROLE

06 BED LINENS

A—
L'AMOUR
Choose colors as bold as
your love!

L'Amour est un bouquet de Violettes

B—

SWEET NOTHINGS

Surround yourself and your loved
ones with whispered messages to
infuse your dreams.

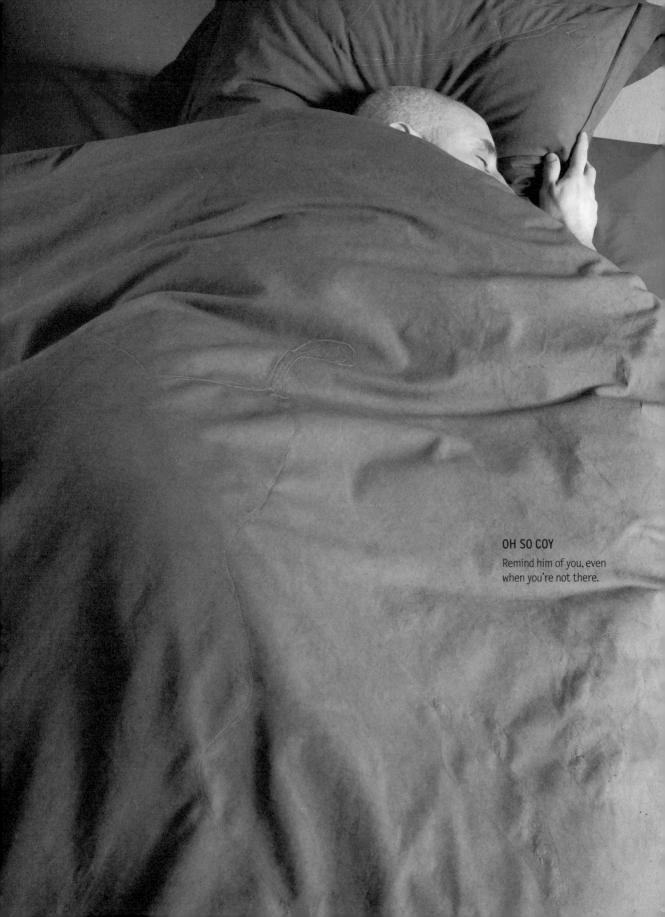

OH SO COY

Remind him of you, even
when you're not there.

06 BED LINENS

D —
GRAPHIC CHERRIES
...over a bed of hot pink polka dots.

06 BED LINENS

WHICHEVER PROJECT YOU CHOOSE,
ALWAYS START BY SOAKING THE
SHEETS AND/OR PILLOWCASES
OVERNIGHT IN COLD WATER BEFORE
MACHINE WASHING THEM TO ENSURE
THE FABRIC WILL NOT SHRINK AFTER
IT HAS BEEN CUSTOMIZED.

A—

L'AMOUR

• 1 DUVET COVER OR TOP SHEET AND
2 PILLOWCASES
• BRIGHT PINK FABRIC DYE (OPTIONAL;
WE USED DYLON FUCHSIA NO. 29)

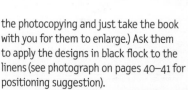

Dye the bed linens if desired, following
manufacturer's instructions on the dye
package. Let dry.
Photocopy the lettering opposite at 450
percent. You may have to do the copying in
several stages to print it that large, or find
a store that specializes in photocopying
large formats. Photocopy the asterisks on
this page at 200 percent.
Take the linens and your copies to an
imaging center. (It may be easier to skip

the photocopying and just take the book
with you for them to enlarge.) Ask them
to apply the designs in black flock to the
linens (see photograph on pages 40–41 for
positioning suggestion).
The finished linens can be machine washed
but must be ironed on the reverse side.

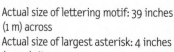

Actual size of lettering motif: 39 inches
(1 m) across
Actual size of largest asterisk: 4 inches
(10 cm) diameter

B—
SWEET NOTHINGS

- 1 DUVET COVER OR TOP SHEET AND 2 PILLOWCASES
- 4-5 YDS (4 M) OF IRON-ON FABRIC NAME LABELS IN A CONTINUOUS ROLL
- IRON
- WHITE THREAD (OPTIONAL)
- SEWING MACHINE (OPTIONAL)

Order a continuous roll of iron-on name labels with a personal message, such as "Good Night, Sweetheart." (See page 63 for suggested resources.)
Iron the duvet cover and pillowcases carefully and lay them on a flat surface. Position the strip of printed labels across the width of the duvet cover or sheet, about 32 inches (80 cm) from the top edge. Cover with a damp cloth and iron to attach the strip.
Repeat for the pillowcases, positioning the strip horizontally on one and vertically on the other, but slightly off center.
For added attachment security, run a line of machine stitching along the edges of each strip.

C—
OH SO COY

- 1 DUVET COVER OR TOP SHEET AND
2 PILLOWCASES
- GRAY FABRIC DYE (OPTIONAL;
WE USED DYLON STEEL GRAY NO. 32)
- IRON-ON TRANSFER PEN
(AVAILABLE AT CRAFT STORES)
- STRAIGHT PINS
- IRON
- BRIGHT PINK THREAD
- SEWING MACHINE

Dye the linens if desired, following
manufacturer's instructions on the dye
package.

Photocopy the clothing design opposite,
enlarged to life size (or whatever size you
want). You can either do this yourself or
go to a copy center and have it done
there.

Trace the outline of your life-size design
with an iron-on transfer pen.

Pin the iron-on design in place, face
down, onto your duvet cover or sheet
and follow manufacturer's directions to
iron the design onto the fabric. Remove
the papers.

Using bright pink thread, sew stitching
around the outline of the design. To make
the outline thicker, repeat two more
times, loosely stitching the same outline
but with slight variation.

Repeat the process on the pillowcases.

D—
GRAPHIC CHERRIES

- 1 DUVET COVER OR TOP SHEET AND
2 PILLOWCASES
- PIECE OF THIN CARDBOARD, APPROX.
9 x 10 in (23 x 26 cm)
- BLACK FABRIC PAINT (WE USED DYLON
BLACK NO. 11)
- REPOSITIONABLE SPRAY ADHESIVE
- CRAFT KNIFE
- MASKING TAPE
- 2 FABRIC PAINT PENS IN BRIGHT PINK
- STENCIL BRUSH OR SPONGE
- IRON

Iron the cover and pillowcases carefully.
Photocopy the cherry design on page 16
at 115 percent. Use spray adhesive to
attach the copy to your cardboard.
Carefully cut out the inside of the cherries
using a craft knife.

Place the stencil on one of the pillowcases
and anchor with masking tape. Use a brush
to apply fabric paint inside the stencil,
using light dabbing motions. Don't
overload the brush or the paint will bleed
under the stencil. Remove the stencil
before the paint is completely dry.

Repeat with the other pillowcase. Let dry
thoroughly, then place a clean piece of
fabric over the design and press with a
hot iron for 2 minutes to fix the design.
The finished pillowcases can be machine
washed. For the duvet cover or sheet, use
fabric paint pens to apply random dots,
placing them close together at the bottom
of the cover and gradually spacing them
more widely toward the top.

Actual size of cherry design: 7½ inches
(19 cm)

LITTLE RED RIDING HOOD
Create a pair of fairy-tale jackets for you and your favorite little person *en français*. The only question is, who gets to be Little Red Riding Hood and who gets to be the Big Bad Wolf?

07 JACKETS

B —

LA VIE EN ROSE BROOCH

Those little scraps of cotton fabric you have lying around will finally get a
higher purpose: accessorizing a favorite old jacket with a splash of color.

C —

FLEA MARKET PINS

A great way to recycle odd earrings, bits of broken jewelry, charms—any treasured trinkets that need a second home.

07 JACKETS

A —

LITTLE RED RIDING HOOD

- 2 SCRAPS OF FABRIC, ONE 14 x 4 in.
(35 x 10 cm) FOR ADULT, AND ONE
10 x 4 in. (25 x 10 cm) FOR CHILD
- 2 COTTON JACKETS, ONE FOR ADULT
AND ONE FOR CHILD
- BRIGHTLY COLORED THREAD
- FABRIC SCISSORS
- SEWING MACHINE

Cut 2 rectangles out of your fabric in the
sizes noted above. When you've decided
which of you will be Little Red Riding Hood
(le petit chaperon rouge) and which the
Big Bad Wolf *(le grand méchant loup)*, take
the fabric rectangles to an imaging center
and ask them to transfer the phrases
shown here at 125 percent.
Sew the rectangles to the backs of the
jackets with two rows of machine stitches
about ½ inch (12 mm) apart and ¼ inch
(6 mm) from the edge of the fabric,
leaving the edges raw.

Actual sizes of the phrases: 10¼ and
9 inches (26 and 23 cm) long

B—

LA VIE EN ROSE BROOCH

- SCRAPS OF FABRIC IN AT LEAST TWO DIFFERENT SHADES OR PATTERNS
- DRAWING COMPASS
- STRAIGHT PINS AND SAFETY PIN
- SEWING NEEDLE
- BRIGHTLY COLORED THREAD
- FABRIC SCISSORS
- SEWING MACHINE

Using the compass and template at right, cut 5 circles out of your fabric, with diameters measuring 1½ in., 2½ in., 3 in., 4 in., and 4¾ in. (4, 6, 8, 10, and 12 cm). Stack the circles by size, with the biggest on the bottom, and pin them together in the center.

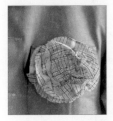

Sew random lines of machine stitching across the circles, making little tucks in the fabric as you go. Sew a safety pin to the back of the brooch by hand.

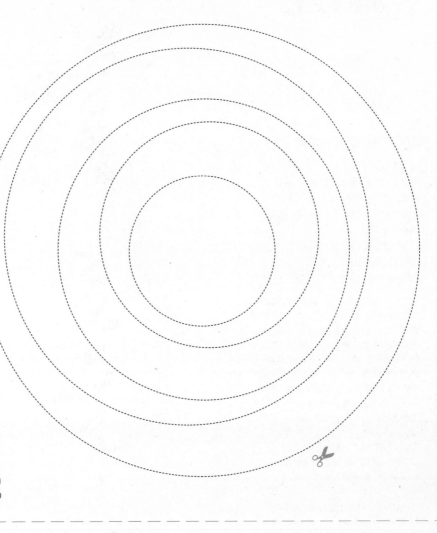

C—

FLEA MARKET PINS

- SMALL PERSONAL MEMENTOS (RIBBON FROM YOUR FAVORITE DRESS AS A CHILD, YOUR BABY BRACELET, LUCKY CHARMS, ODD EARRINGS, ETC.)
- JUMP RINGS (FOUND AT CRAFT AND BEADING STORES)
- JEWELRY PLIERS
- EXTRA-LARGE SAFETY PIN (1 PER FINISHED PIN)
- SEWING NEEDLE AND THREAD (OPTIONAL)

Use the pliers to attach jump rings to your little mementos, then attach them to the shank of the safety pin. Anchor ribbons or fabric scraps with a few stitches.

A—

PERFECT PATCHES

Whether or not your clothes are frayed at the elbows, give them a vintage feel with these pretty layered patches.

B —

VIVE LA HANDKERCHIEF

Go green by giving up tissues and
leading a revival of cotton
handkerchiefs! It'll be easy when
you have hankies as cute as these.

09 SHOES

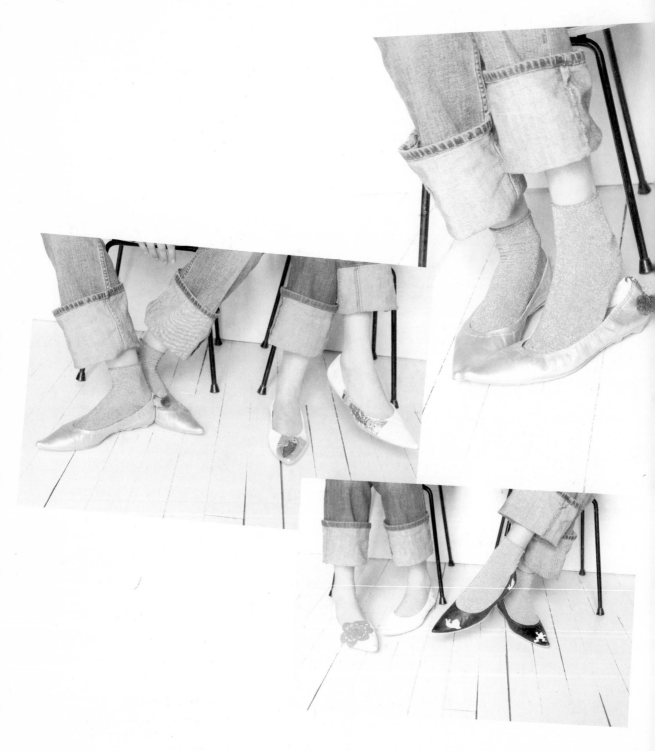

MY FUNKY FLATS

Expose your sole: Transform plain flats into shoes with one-of-a-kind character.

o8 HANDKERCHIEFS

A—
PRETTY PATCHES

- 2 LARGE PATTERNED HANDKERCHIEFS
- DRAWING COMPASS
- STRAIGHT PINS
- MATCHING THREAD
- SEWING NEEDLE
- FABRIC SCISSORS
- SEWING MACHINE

Use the compass to trace five circles onto one handkerchief, with diameters of 1½ in., 2½ in., 3 in., 4 in., and 4¾ in. (4, 6, 8, 10, and 12 cm). Cut out the circles.
Stack the circles from biggest to smallest and pin them together in the center. Sew around the edge of each circle with a line of machine stitches, leaving the edges raw. Sew two rows of stitches across the center of the patch to form a cross.
Pin the patch onto the elbow of your garment and sew in place by hand.
Repeat for the other patch.

B—
VIVE LA HANDKERCHIEF

- HANDKERCHIEF
- FABRIC PAINT
- REPOSITIONABLE SPRAY ADHESIVE
- PIECE OF THIN CARDBOARD
- CRAFT KNIFE
- MASKING TAPE
- STENCIL BRUSH OR SPONGE
- IRON

Photocopy the design shown here at actual size. Use spray adhesive to attach the copy to your cardboard. Carefully cut out the inside of the letters with a craft knife to make a stencil.

Position the stencil on your handkerchief and secure with masking tape. Use a brush to apply fabric paint over the stencil, using light dabbing motions.

When the paint is almost dry, remove the stencil. Let dry entirely, then cover with a piece of plain fabric and fix the design by pressing with a hot iron for 2 minutes.

09 SHOES

C—
POM-POMS

- PAIR OF LEATHER FLATS
- LEATHER SHOE DYE IN SILVER (OPTIONAL)
- 6 POM-POMS IN DIFFERENT COLORS
- SEWING NEEDLE SUITABLE FOR LEATHER
- STRONG THREAD

If desired, dye your shoes silver, following manufacturer's instructions.
If the pom-poms don't have ties, make your own from a few strands of wool and attach to each pom-pom with a few stitches before sewing three pom-poms to the back of each shoe.

A—
LE ZOO

- PAIR OF LEATHER FLATS
- ANIMAL-SHAPED STICKERS
- LEATHER DYING KIT
- MASKING TAPE
- SPONGE

Prepare the shoes for dyeing according to the manufacturer's instructions.
Position one or two animal stickers on each shoe, making the right shoe different from the left.
Protect the soles with masking tape.
Apply two coats of dye over each shoe, dabbing it on gently with a sponge.
Remove the stickers carefully before the dye is completely dry. Remove the masking tape and let dry overnight before wearing.

B—
SWEET FEET

- PAIR OF LEATHER FLATS
- FOIL CANDY WRAPPERS WITH FUN PATTERNS
- CLEAR, WEATHERPROOF LEATHER VARNISH
- PAINTBRUSH

Eat the candy. Position the empty, clean candy wrappers on both shoes.
Brush a coat of varnish underneath the wrappers, attach to each shoe, and let dry. Apply 2–3 coats of varnish on top of the wrappers. Let dry completely before wearing.

D—
DOILY D.I.Y.

- PAIR OF LEATHER FLATS
- 2 CLOTH DOILIES, EACH APPROX. 3½ in. (9 cm) IN DIAMETER
- 2 CANS OF FLUORESCENT SPRAY PAINT (1 YELLOW AND 1 PINK)
- SEWING NEEDLE SUITABLE FOR LEATHER
- STRONG THREAD

Spray-paint one doily pink and the other yellow. Make sure you do the spraying outside or in a well-ventilated room while wearing a face mask, and protect the floor or work surface with plenty of old newspaper. Let the doilies dry thoroughly. Sew the doilies to the side of one shoe, layering the pink doily over the yellow one. Leave the other shoe plain.